PIANO · VOCAL · GUITAR

Groovy Years

53 Songs of the Hippie Era

This publication is not for sale in
the E.C. and/or Australia
or New Zealand.

ISBN 0-7935-5059-9

HAL·LEONARD
CORPORATION

7777 W. BLUEMOUND RD. P.O. BOX 13819 MILWAUKEE, WI 53213

The Groovy Years
53 Songs of the Hippie Era

● ● ● ● ● ● ● ●

CONTENTS

miniskirts/maxiskirts
the midi/unisex

THE ESTABLISHMENT IS ALIVE AND WELL IN WASHINGTON
(ART BUCHWALD)

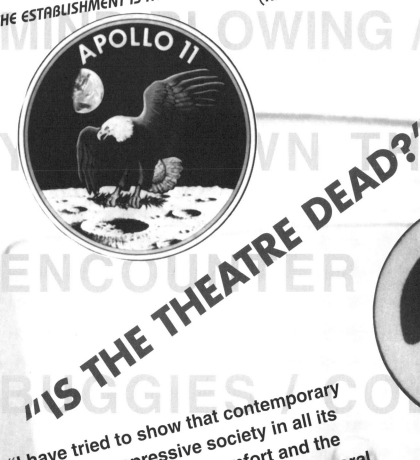

"If you want to join the New York intellectual establishment... all you've got to do is make the right friends and then attack them, claim that the establishment doesn't exist and that everyone in it is brilliant, and denounce the mass media while they are lionizing you.""

-VICTOR S. NAVASKY

KICKY

"IS THE THEATRE DEAD?"

"I have tried to show that contemporary society is a repressive society in all its aspects, that even the comfort and the prosperity, the alleged political and moral freedom, are utilized for repressive ends."

- Herbert Marcuse

GO-GO BOOTS

"JUST WHEN YOU THINK YOU'RE GETTING FAMOUS, SOMEBODY COMES ALONG AND MAKES YOU LOOK LIKE A WARM-UP ACT FOR AMATEUR NIGHT...POPE PAUL VI [FOR EXAMPLE]. TALK ABOUT ADVANCE PR — I MEAN FOR CENTURIES."

-ANDY WARHOL

JOHNSON FOR EX-PRESIDENT

"I know that probably most of you think I'm an S.O.B., but I want you to know I understand just how you feel."
-Richard Nixon, to student demonstrators

ROD McKUEN
LISTEN TO THE WARM

THE AUTOBIOGRAPHY OF MALCOLM X

"This is not a bedroom war. This is a political movement."
-Betty Friedan

I'm a Plainclothes Hippie

The Electric Kool-Aid Acid Test
(Tom Wolfe)

"DROP OUT, TURN ON, TUNE IN."
-Timothy Leary,
The Psychedelic Reader

FLOWER POWER

TODAY EAST VILLAGE TOMORROW THE WORLD

LOVE POWER

"Why does integration have to begin with our children?"
-Anonymous, quoted in *The New York Times*

LEATHER
TUNICS
HYPE
OVERALLS
VESTS
PEASANT DRESSES
ARMY-NAVY SURPLUS
EMBROIDERED WORK SHIRTS
NEHRU JACKET
CARNABY STREET
HIP HUGGERS
WIDE TIES
TURTLENECKS
FISH NETS
TOPLESS
BELL SLEEVES
TIE-DYE

THE PROPHET
KAHLIL GIBRAN

INTEGRATION

Games People Play
(Eric Berne)

ROWAN AND MARTIN'S LAUGH-IN

HAIR   (Ganshaw & Prescott)

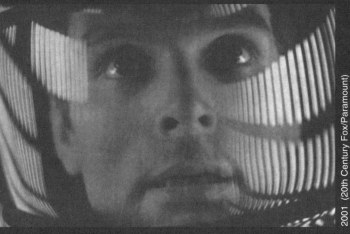

"We came, therefore (and with many Western thinkers before us), to suspect civilization may be overvalued."

-Gary Snyder

(Friedman-Abels)

OH CALCUTTA!

FLICKS / NUDE / STEPPENWOLF / ROCK OPERA / VIOLENCE / SUSAN SONTAG

gurus
PSYCHEDELIC

BLOW-UP (MGM/UA)

BONNIE & CLYDE (Warner Bros.)

"[Pop Art] the use of commercial art as a subject matter in painting...It was hard to get a painting that was despicable enough so that no one would hang it...The one thing everyone hated was commercial art; apparently they didn't hate that enough either."
-Roy Lichtenstein

UNDERGROUND

LOVE BEADS HAIR

THE HUMAN BE-IN

threads / the afro / jumpsuits

SANDALS

"THE MEDIUM IS THE MESSAGE."
-MARSHALL McLUHAN

"Once it was power that created style. But now high styles come from low places, from people who have no power...who are marginal, who carve out worlds for themselves in the nether depths, in tainted 'undergrounds.'
-Tom Wolfe,
"Girl of the Year"

CONCEPT ALBUM / ROD McKUEN / THE DOORS / FOLK-ROCK / FILM AS POLITICS / A
JIMI HENDRIX / JACQUELINE SUSANN / MOVIE RATINGS / THE WHO / THE ROLLING STON
FELLINI / WOODSTOCK / ALTAMONT / KURT VONNEGUT / SURREAL

HAIGHT PEACE

"There [in Haight-Ashbury], in a daily street-fair atmosphere, upwards of 15,000 unbonded girls and boys interact in a tribal love-seeking, free-winging, acid-based society, where if you are a hippie and you have a dime, you can put it in a parking meter and lie down in the street for an hour's sunshine."
-Warren Hinkle, *Social History of the Hippies*

BELL BOTTOMS

YIPPIE / SIT-IN / SDS / THE DRAFT / VIETNAM / PEACE MARCH / DEMONSTRATION / ASSASINATION

the body stocking

FROSTED LIPSTICK

PLASTIC JEWELRY

RUDY GERNREICH

PANTS SUIT

KENT STATE

BLACK POWER

bikini

LIBERATION

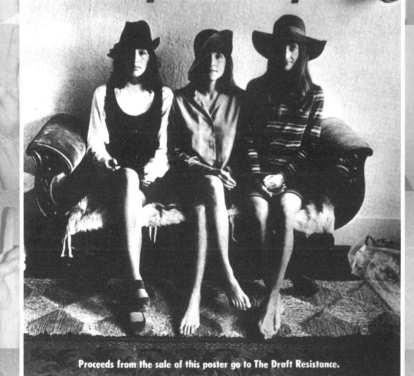

GIRLS SAY YES
to boys who say NO

Proceeds from the sale of this poster go to The Draft Resistance.

Anti-draft week
MARCH 16-22

"I DON'T SEE AN AMERICAN DREAM...I SEE AN AMERICAN NIGHTMARE...THREE HUNDRED AND TEN YEARS WE WORKED IN THIS COUNTRY WITHOUT A DIME IN RETURN."

-MALCOLM X

Abraham, Martin And John

Words and Music by
RICHARD HOLLER

All You Need Is Love

Words and Music by JOHN LENNON
and PAUL McCARTNEY

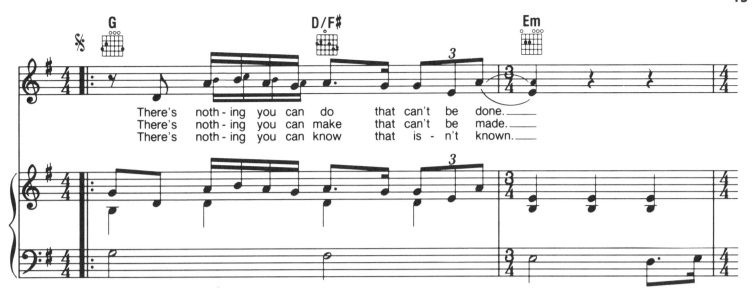

There's noth-ing you can do that can't be done.___
There's noth-ing you can make that can't be made.___
There's noth-ing you can know that is-n't known.___

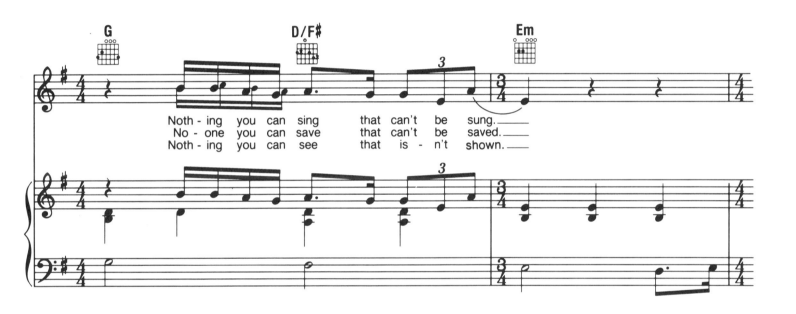

Noth-ing you can sing that can't be sung.___
No-one you can save that can't be saved.___
Noth-ing you can see that is-n't shown.___

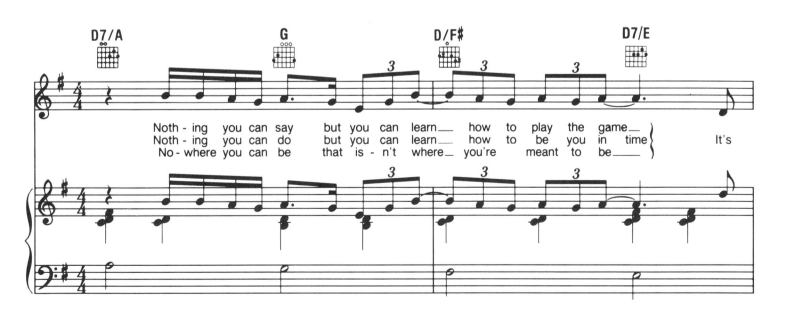

Noth-ing you can say but you can learn___ how to play the game___
Noth-ing you can do but you can learn___ how to be you in time
No-where you can be that is-n't where___ you're meant to be___

It's

Because

Words and Music by JOHN LENNON
and PAUL McCARTNEY

Be - cause the world is round, it turns me
cause the wind is high, it blows my
cause the sky is blue, it makes me

And When I Die

Words and Music by
LAURA NYRO

Blackbird

Words and Music by JOHN LENNON
and PAUL McCARTNEY

Black - bird sing-ing in the dead of night___
Black - bird sing-ing in the dead of night___

Take these bro-ken wings___ and learn to fly;___
Take these sunk-en eyes___ and learn to see;___

All your life_____ you were on-ly wait-ing for this mo-ment to a -
All your life_____ you were on-ly wait-ing for this mo-ment to be

Born To Be Wild

Words and Music by
MARS BONFIRE

California Dreamin'

Words and Music by JOHN PHILLIPS
and MICHELLE PHILLIPS

Medium Rock beat

MCA music publishing

Come Together

Moderately slow, with a double-time feeling

Words and Music by JOHN LENNON
and PAUL McCARTNEY

Here come old flat-top, He come groov-ing up slow-ly, He got Joo Joo eye-ball, He one

ho - ly roll - er, He got hair down to his knee.__

Got to be a jok - er, He just do what he please.__

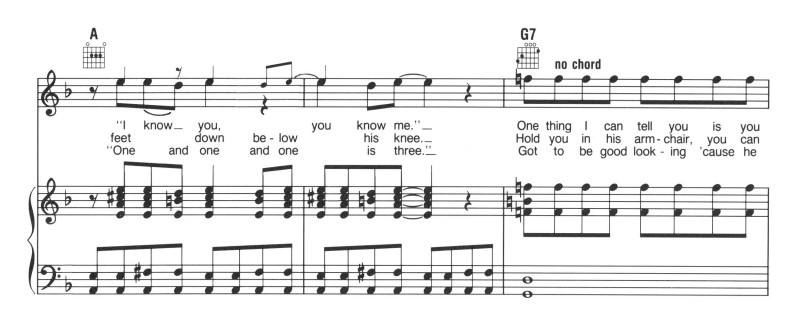

Creeque Alley

Words and Music by JOHN PHILLIPS
and M. GILLIAM

Additional Lyrics

3. When Cass was a sophomore,
   planned to go to Swarthmore,
   but she changed her mind one day.
   Standin' on the turnpike
   thumb out to hitchhike,
   take her to New York right away.
   When Denny met Cass he gave her love bumps,
   called John and Zal and that was the Mugwumps.
   McGuinn and McGuire couldn't get no higher,
   but that's what they were aimin' at,
   and no one's gettin' fat except Mama Cass.

4. Mugwumps, high jumps, slow slumps, big bumps.
   Don't you work as hard as you play?
   Make-up, break-up, ev'rything you shake up,
   guess it had to be that way.
   Sebastian and Zal formed a Spoonful;
   Michelle, John and Denny gettin' very tuneful.
   McGuinn and McGuire just a-catchin' fire.
   In L.A. you know where that's at.
   And everybody's gettin' fat except Mama Cass.
   Do do do do do do, do do do do, woh.

5. Broke, busted, disgusted, agents can't be trusted;
   and then she wants to go to the sea.
   Cass can't make it. She says, "We'll have to fake it."
   We knew she'd come eventually.
   Greasin' on American Express card,
   Tents, low rent and keepin' out the heat's hard
   Duffy's good vibrations and our imaginations
   can't go on indefinitely,
   and California Dreamin' is becoming a reality.

Different Drum

Words and Music by
MICHAEL NESMITH

Eve Of Destruction

Words and Music by
P.F. SLOAN

Moderately, with intensity

1. The East - ern world it is ex - plod - in',
3., 4. *See additional lyrics*

vi - o -lence flar - in' and bul - lets load - in'. You're old e-nough to kill, but

not for __ vot - in', You don't be - lieve in war, but what's that gun you're to - tin'? And

Additional Lyrics

3. My blood's so mad feels like coagulatin'
    I'm sittin' here just contemplatin'
    You can't twist the truth it knows no regulatin'
    And a handful of Senators don't pass legislation
    Marches alone can't bring integration
    When human respect is disintegratin'
    This whole crazy world is just too frustatin'.
    (To Chorus:)

4. Think of all the hate there is in Red China
    Then take a look around to Selma, Alabama!
    You may leave here for four days in space
    But when you return, it's the same old place,
    The pounding drums, the pride and disgrace
    You can bury your dead, but don't leave a trace
    Hate your next door neighbor, but don't forget to say grace.
    (To Chorus:)

Everybody's Talkin'
(Echoes)

Words and Music by
FRED NEIL

54

skip-pin' o - ver the o - cean like a stone.

D.S. al Coda

CODA

And

I won't let you leave my love ___ be - hind.

Repeat and Fade

And

Give Peace A Chance

Words and Music by JOHN LENNON
and PAUL McCARTNEY

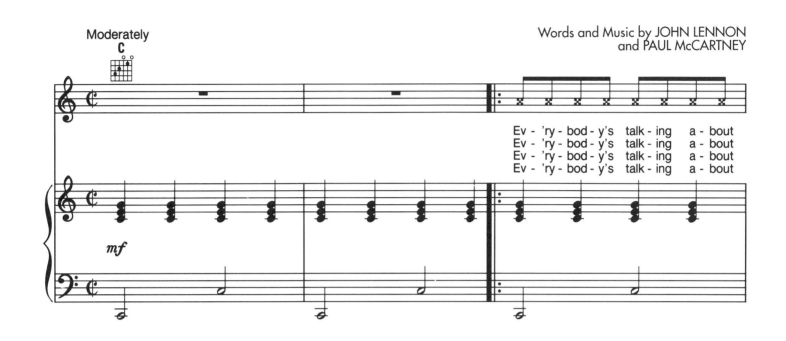

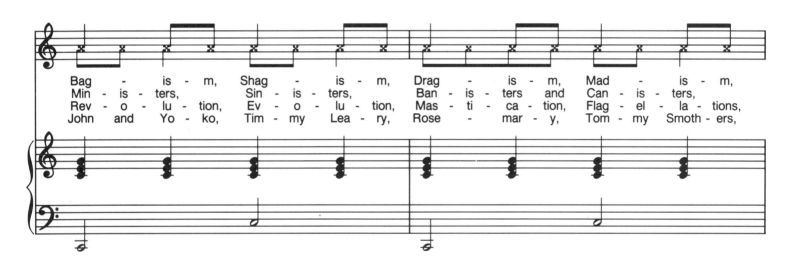

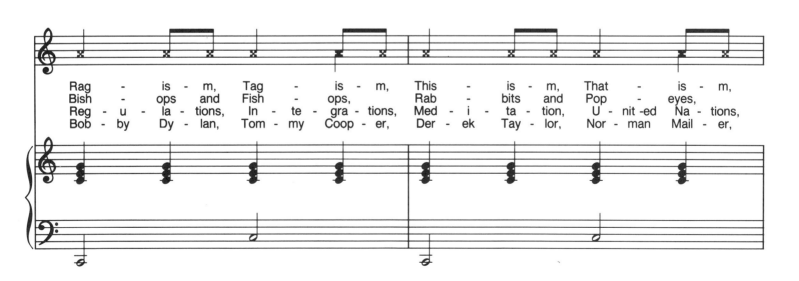

Is - n't it the most?
Bye - bye   Bye-byes.
Con - grad - u - la - tions.
Al - len Gins-berg, Ha - re Krish - na Ha - re, Ha - re Krish - na.

All   we___ are

say   -   ing___   is give peace___ a

chance._____   All   we___ are

say   -   ing___   is give peace___ a

For Your Love

Words and Music by
GRAHAM GOULDMAN

Groovin'

Words and Music by FELIX CAVALIERE
and EDWARD BRIGATI, JR.

Moderately slow

Groov - in' _____ on a Sun - day af - ter - noon. _____
Groov - in' _____ down a crowd - ed a - ve - nue. _____
Groov - in' _____ on a Sun - day af - ter - noon. _____

Real - ly _____ could - n't get a - way too
Do - in' _____ an - y - thing we'd like to
Real - ly _____ could - n't get a - way too

soon. _____
do. _____

I can't im - ag - ine an - y -
There's al - ways lots of things that

Helter Skelter

Words and Music by JOHN LENNON
and PAUL McCARTNEY

When I get to the bot-tom I go

back to the top of the slide,__ Where I stop and I turn, and I go for a ride,__

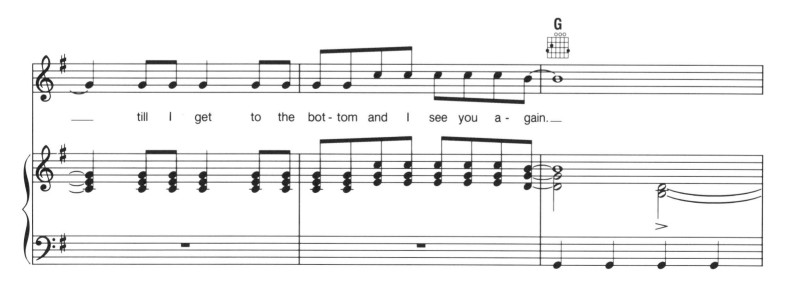

__ till I get to the bot-tom and I see you a-gain.__

A Groovy Kind Of Love

Words and Music by TONI WINE
and CAROLE BAYER SAGER

Slowly

When I'm feel-in' blue, all I have to do is take a look at
want to, you can turn me on to an-y-thing you

you, then I'm not so _____ blue. When you're close to me,
want to, an-y-time at _____ all. When I kiss your lips,

I can feel your
oo, I start to

Happy Together

Words and Music by GARRY BONNER
and ALAN GORDON

He Ain't Heavy...He's My Brother

Words and Music by BOB RUSSELL
and BOBBY SCOTT

Moderately slow, with feeling

mp

with pedal throughout

Bb   **F**   **Eb**   **F7**

long   with man - y a wind - ing turn,   that leads   us to
go,   his wel - fare is my con - cern.   No bur - den is
road,   from which there is no re - turn.   While we're   on our

Gm   **Ab**   **F11**

who   knows   where,   who knows   where.   But   I'm
he   to   bear,   we'll get   there.   For   I
way   to   there,   why not   share?   And   the

Bbmaj7   **F**   **Eb**

strong,_____   strong e - nough   to   car - ry him.   He Ain't
know_____   he would not   en - cum - ber me.__   He Ain't
load_____   does - n't weigh   me down   at all.__   He Ain't

Here Comes The Sun

Words and Music by
GEORGE HARRISON

Here comes ___ the sun, ___

Here comes ___ the sun, ___ and I say, "It's all ___ right."

Sun,   sun,   sun,   here it

comes.

Hey Joe

Words and Music by
BILLY ROBERTS

I Am The Walrus

Words and Music by JOHN LENNON
and PAUL McCARTNEY

Slow 4

I am he as you are he as you are me and we are all to-geth-er__
Ex-pert tex-pert chok-ing smok-ers, don't you think the jok-er laughs at you?__

-er____

See how they run, like pigs from a gun, see how__
See how they smile, like pigs in a sty, see how__

Imagine

Words and Music by
JOHN LENNON

I Can See For Miles

Words and Music by
PETER TOWNSHEND

I know you've de-ceived me. Now here's a sur-prise.

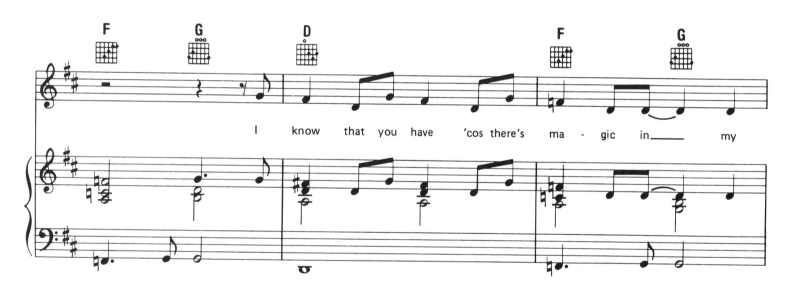

I know that you have 'cos there's ma-gic in____ my

eyes. I can see for miles and miles and

It's Your Thing

By RUDOLPH ISLEY, RONALD ISLEY
and O'KELLY ISLEY

To Coda

Lay Down
(Candles In The Rain)

Words and Music by
MELANIE SAFKA

Slow Gospel Rock

Lay down, lay down, lay it all down, let your white birds smile up at the

ones who stand and frown. Lay down, lay down, lay it all down, let your

white birds smile up at the ones who stand and frown.

Repeat and Fade

Leaving On A Jet Plane

Words and Music by
JOHN DENVER

Let's Live For Today

Words and Music by GUIDO CENCIARELLI,
GIULIO RAPETTI and NORMAN DAVID

Love Is All Around

Words and Music by
REG PRESLEY

Lucy In The Sky With Diamonds

Words and Music by JOHN LENNON
and PAUL McCARTNEY

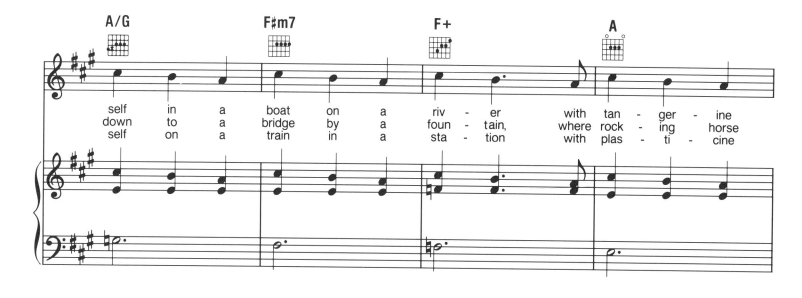

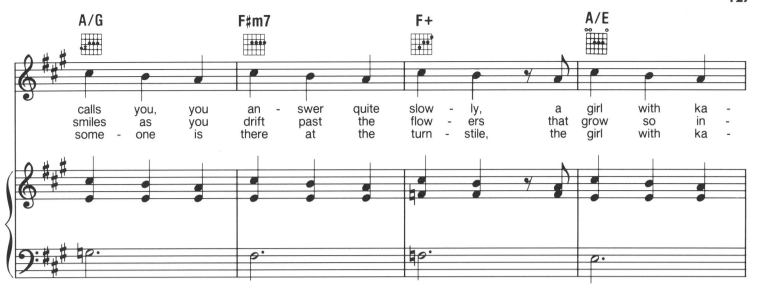

calls you, you an - swer quite slow - ly, a girl with ka -
smiles as you drift past the flow - ers that grow so in -
some - one is there at the turn - stile, the girl with ka -

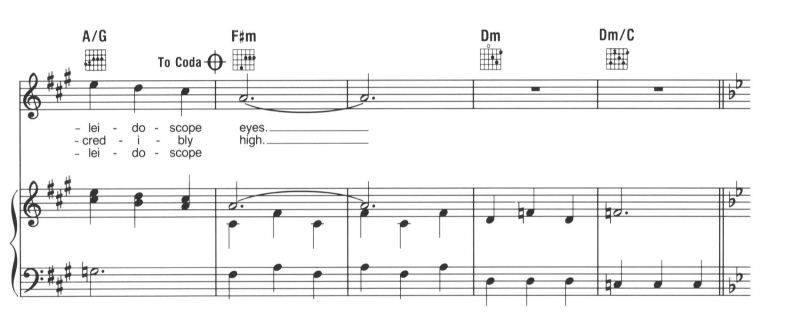

To Coda

- lei - do - scope eyes.
- cred - i - bly high.
- lei - do - scope

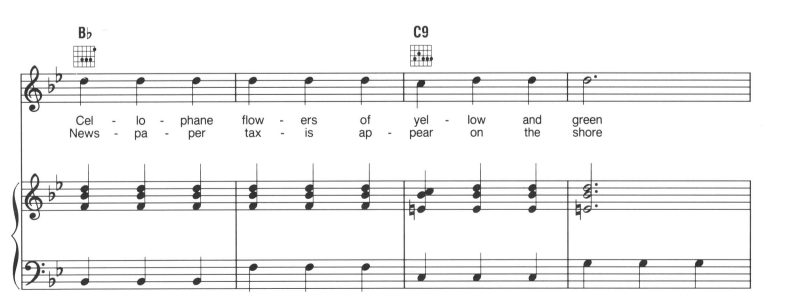

Cel - lo - phane flow - ers of yel - low and green
News - pa - per tax - is ap - pear on the shore

The Magic Bus

Words and Music by
PETER TOWNSHEND

Magic Carpet Ride

Words and Music by JOHN KAY
and RUSHTON MOREVE

Me And Bobby McGee

Words and Music by KRIS KRISTOFFERSON
and FRED FOSTER

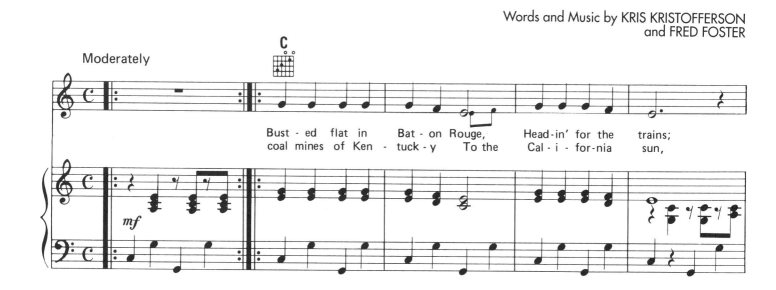

Moderately

Bust-ed flat in Bat-on Rouge, Head-in' for the trains;
coal mines of Ken-tuck-y To the Cal-i-for-nia sun,

Feel-in' near-ly fad-ed as my jeans,
Bob-by shared the se-crets of my soul;

Bob-by thumbed a
Stand-in' right be-

die-sel down just be-fore it rained; Took us all the
side me, Lord, Through ev-ery-thing I done, And ev-ery night she

Mississippi Queen

Words and Music by LESLIE WEST, FELIX PAPPALARDI,
CORKY LAING and DAVID REA

Nights In White Satin

Words and Music by
JUSTIN HAYWARD

C
1
Em
love you,
Oh, how I love you.
f
D
Em
D
2
Em
D
Em
love you.
Oh, how I love
D
Em
Em7
you.
mp

Piece Of My Heart

Words and Music by JERRY RAGOVOY
and BERT BERNS

Slowly with a beat

Did-n't I make you feel like you were the on - ly man,

Did-n't I give you ev-'ry-thing that a wom-an pos-si-bly can,

But with all the love I give you, it's nev-er e-nough,__ But

You're out in the street look-in' good, __ And you know deep down
in your heart that ain't right, ___ And, oh _____ you
nev-er, nev-er hear me when I cry at night, __ Woh-oh - oh, __
I tell my-self that I can't stand the pain, But when you
hold me in your arms I say it a-gain. __ So

D.S. al Fine

One Toke Over The Line

Words and Music by MICHAEL BREWER
and THOMAS E. SHIPLEY

People Got To Be Free

Words and Music by FELIX CAVALIERE
and EDWARD BRIGATI, JR.

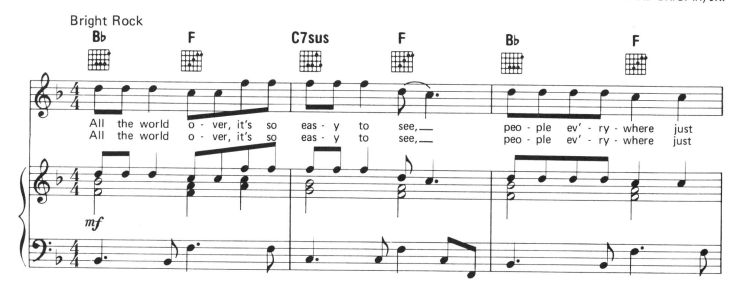

Revolution

Words and Music by JOHN LENNON
and PAUL McCARTNEY

Moderate Rock and Roll Shuffle

C

You   say you want a rev - o - lu -
say you got a real so - lu -
say you'll change the con - sti - tu -

F

- tion, _____ Well _____ you know, _____   We all want _____
- tion, _____ Well _____ you know, _____   We'd all love _____
- tion, _____ Well _____ you know, _____   We all want _____

to change the world.
to see the plan.
to change your head.

You
You
You

tell me that it's e - vo - lu - tion, _____ Well _____ you know, _____
ask me for a con - tri - bu - tion, _____ Well _____ you know, _____
tell me it's the in - sti - tu - tion, _____ Well _____ you know, _____

We all want _____ to change the world. _____
We're all do - ing what we can. _____
You better free _____ your mind in - stead. _____

Rock Me
from the film CANDY

Words and Music by
JOHN KAY

Strawberry Fields Forever

Words and Music by JOHN LENNON
and PAUL McCARTNEY

Let me take you down ___ 'cause I'm go - in' to ___ Straw - ber - ry

Fields. Noth - ing is real, and noth - ing to get hung a - bout.

Straw - ber - ry Fields ___ for - ev - er. ___

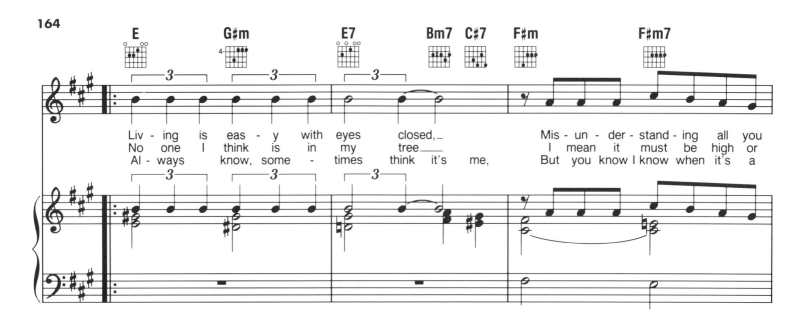

San Francisco
(Be Sure To Wear Some Flowers In Your Hair)

Words and Music by
JOHN PHILLIPS

Spinning Wheel

Words and Music by
DAVID CLAYTON THOMAS

Moderately slow, with a beat

What goes up must come down, Spin-ning Wheel

got to go 'round.— Talk-in' 'bout your trou-bles, it's a cry-in' sin,—

Stoned Soul Picnic
(Picnic, A Green City)

Words and Music by
LAURA NYRO

Strange Brew

Words and Music by ERIC CLAPTON,
FELIX PAPPALARDI and GAIL COLLINS

Summer In The City

Words and Music by JOHN SEBASTIAN,
STEVE BOONE and MARK SEBASTIAN

Moderately, with a steady beat

Hot town, sum-mer in the cit-y, back o' my neck get-ting dirt-y and grit-ty.
Cool town, eve-nin' in the cit-y, dressed so fine and a look-in' so pret-ty.

Instrumental to Fade

Been down, is-n't it a pit-y. Does-n't seem to be a shad-ow in the cit-y.
Cool cat, look-in' for a kit-ty. Gon-na look in ev'-ry cor-ner of the cit-y.

All a-round, peo-ple look-in' half dead, Walk-in' on the side-walk hot-ter than a match, yeah.
Till_ I'm wheez-in' like a bus stop. Run-nin' up the stairs, gon-na meet you on the roof-top.__

The Sunshine Of Your Love

Words and Music by JACK BRUCE,
PETE BROWN and ERIC CLAPTON

Well, it's get - ting near dawn __
I'm with you my love, ___

when lights close their tired_____ eyes.__
the light shin - ing through___ on___ you.__

I've been wait -

- ing so ____ long to be where ____ I'm go - ing ____

in the sun - shine of __ your love. ____

Sweet Baby James

Words and Music by
JAMES TAYLOR

Turn! Turn! Turn!
(To Everything There Is A Season)

Words from the Book of Ecclesiastes
Adaptation and Music by PETE SEEGER

White Room

Words and Music by JACK BRUCE
and PETE BROWN

A Whiter Shade Of Pale

Words and Music by KEITH REID
and GARY BROOKER

We skipped the light fan-dan-go, turned cart-wheels 'cross the
She said, "I'm home on shore leave," though in truth we were at
She said,"There is no rea-son, and the truth is plain to

floor; I was feel-ing kind of sea-sick,
sea; So I took her by the look-ing glass
see," But I wan-dered through my play-ing cards

Wild Thing

Words and Music by
CHIP TAYLOR

Workin' On A Groovy Thing

Words and Music by NEIL SEDAKA
and ROGER ATKINS

Contemporary Classics

Your favorite songs for piano, voice and guitar.

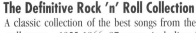

The Definitive Rock 'n' Roll Collection

A classic collection of the best songs from the early rock 'n' roll years – 1955-1966. 97 songs, including: Barbara Ann • Chantilly Lace • Dream Lover • Duke Of Earl • Earth Angel • Great Balls Of Fire • Louie, Louie • Rock Around The Clock • Ruby Baby • Runaway • (Seven Little Girls) Sitting In The Back Seat • Stay • Surfin' U.S.A. • Wild Thing • Woolly Bully • and more.

00490195 ....$24.95

The Big Book Of Rock

78 of rock's biggest hits, including: Addicted To Love • American Pie • Born To Be Wild • Cold As Ice • Dust In The Wind • Free Bird • Goodbye Yellow Brick Road • Groovin' • Hey Jude • I Love Rock N Roll • Lay Down Sally • Layla • Livin' On A Prayer • Louie Louie • Maggie May • Me And Bobby McGee • Monday, Monday • Owner Of A Lonely Heart • Shout • Walk This Way • We Didn't Start The Fire • You Really Got Me • and more.

00311566 ....$19.95

Big Book Of Movie And TV Themes

Over 90 familiar themes, including: Alfred Hitchcock Theme • Beauty And The Beast • Candle On The Water • Theme From *E.T.* • Endless Love • Hawaii Five-O • I Love Lucy • Theme From *Jaws* • Jetsons • Major Dad Theme • The Masterpiece • Mickey Mouse March • The Munsters Theme • Theme From *Murder, She Wrote* • Mystery • Somewhere Out There • Unchained Melody • Won't You Be My Neighbor • and more!

00311582 ....$19.95

The Best Rock Songs Ever

70 of the best rock songs from yesterday and today, including: All Day And All Of The Night • All Shook Up • Ballroom Blitz • Bennie And The Jets • Blue Suede Shoes • Born To Be Wild • Boys Are Back In Town • Every Breath You Take • Faith • Free Bird • Hey Jude • I Still Haven't Found What I'm Looking For • Livin' On A Prayer • Lola • Louie Louie • Maggie May • Money • (She's) Some Kind Of Wonderful • Takin' Care Of Business • Walk This Way • We Didn't Start The Fire • We Got The Beat • Wild Thing • more!

00490424 ....$16.95

The Best Of 90s Rock

30 songs, including: Alive • I'd Do Anything For Love (But I Won't Do That) • Livin' On The Edge • Losing My Religion • Two Princes • Walking On Broken Glass • Wind Of Change • and more.

00311668 ....$14.95

35 Classic Hits

35 contemporary favorites, including: Beauty And The Beast • Dust In The Wind • Just The Way You Are • Moon River • The River Of Dreams • Somewhere Out There • Tears In Heaven • When I Fall In Love • A Whole New World (Aladdin's Theme) • and more.

00311654 ....$12.95

55 Contemporary Standards

55 favorites, including: Alfie • Beauty And The Beast • Can't Help Falling In Love • Candle In The Wind • Have I Told You Lately • How Am I Supposed To Live Without You • Memory • The River Of Dreams • Sea Of Love • Tears In Heaven • Up Where We Belong • When I Fall In Love • and more.

00311670 ....$15.95

The New Grammy® Awards Song Of The Year Songbook

Every song named Grammy Awards' "Song Of The Year" from 1958 to 1988. 28 songs, featuring: Volare • Moon River • The Shadow Of Your Smile • Up, Up and Away • Bridge Over Troubled Water • You've Got A Friend • Killing Me Softly With His Song • The Way We Were • You Light Up My Life • Evergreen • Sailing • Bette Davis Eyes • We Are The World • That's What Friends Are For • Somewhere Out There • Don't Worry, Be Happy.

00359932 ....$12.95

Soft Rock – Revised

39 romantic mellow hits, including: Beauty And The Beast • Don't Know Much • Save The Best For Last • Vision Of Love • Just Once • Dust In The Wind • Just The Way You Are • Your Song.

00311596 ....$14.95

37 Super Hits Of The Superstars

37 big hits by today's most popular artists, including Billy Joel, Amy Grant, Elton John, Rod Stewart, Mariah Carey, Wilson Phillips, Paula Abdul and many more. Songs include: Addicted To Love • Baby Baby • Endless Love • Here And Now • Hold On • Lost In Your Eyes • Love Takes Time • Vision Of Love • We Didn't Start The Fire.

00311539 ....$14.95

FOR MORE INFORMATION, SEE YOUR LOCAL MUSIC DEALER,
OR WRITE TO:

HAL•LEONARD™ CORPORATION

7777 W. BLUEMOUND RD. P.O. BOX 13819 MILWAUKEE, WI 53213

Prices, contents & availability subject to change without notice.